KU-082-105

A PICTURE SCIENCE BOOK

MICHAEL GIBSON

# Digging into the past

*Illustrated by Valerie Bell*

HODDER AND STOUGHTON
LONDON SYDNEY AUCKLAND TORONTO

# CONTENTS



ISBN 0-340-17651-2


First published 1975.
Second impression 1980.



Printed in Great Britain for Hodder and Stoughton Children's Books, a division of Hodder and Stoughton Ltd, Mill Road, Dunton Green, Sevenoaks, Kent TN13 2YJ (Editorial Office: 47 Bedford Square, London WC1B 3DP), by Sackville Press Billericay Ltd

PHOTOGRAPHIC ACKNOWLEDGEMENTS:
3 Paul Popper Ltd; 4 Camera Press; 6 Thomas Photos, Oxford; 7 Aerofilms Ltd; 12 British Museum; 16 Miss B. Wagstaff ARPS; 18 Mansell Collection; 19 Mansell Collection; 23 J Allan Cash Ltd; 25 Radio Times Hulton Picture Library; 29 copyright reserved; 32 Crown copyright

# What is archaeology?

*Right: fossil Shells. The larger is an Ammonite still commonly found in most limestone rocks. This example dates back about 200 million years*

*Far right: the skull of a Neanderthal man, who lived 40,000 years ago*

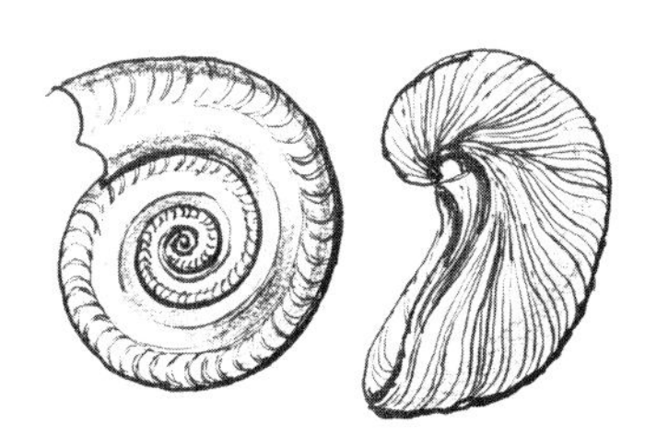

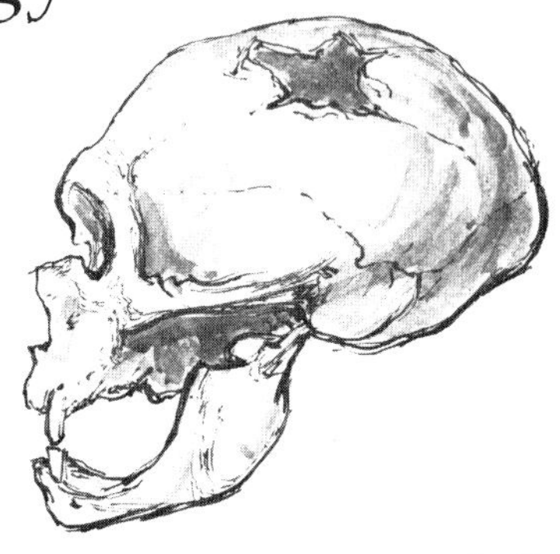

*Detail of a prehistoric rock painting from Southern Rhodesia. This was painted about 5,000 years ago*

Archaeology can be very exciting, but it is not just a search for buried treasure. It can be just as thrilling to discover a bone or a skull which helps to fill in the gaps in our knowledge of the world before history began.

A large part of the work of archaeologists consists in digging to find the remains of old civilisations – temples, palaces, houses or primitive huts. From these, and from exploring caves that once were lived in, one can learn a lot about life thousands and even millions of years ago. Fossils which are found can tell us much about the plants and animals of early days.

But it is of no use finding things if you do not know what they mean and sometimes even what they are. So archaeology also includes studying what you have found, determining how old it is, what it was used for, and making careful records of everything about it. It also means discovering ways of preserving finds, for objects buried for a long time can fall to pieces or decay when exposed once more to the air. There is room in archaeology for writers, scientists, chemists, photographers, labourers, historians, carpenters, surveyors, engineers. But all must have a lot of patience. It is very slow and painstaking work as a rule.

*The Serapeum at Sakara in Egypt, burial place of the sacred bulls, discovered by the Frenchman, Mariette, in 1881*

# How do things from the past get lost or buried?

There are very many ways in which this can happen. At its very simplest, a man in the distant past may have dropped a hunting knife, a coin or other small object. Sand or soil would blow over it, year after year, so that gradually earth would build up over it.

Buildings, if they are deserted, will gradually crumble and fall down, so that over the years soil can blow over them in the same way. In some of the hotter countries in the Middle East, like Egypt and Palestine, winds can blow the dry sand and dust about even more easily. This will pile up against a deserted building, filtering in through window and door openings, and covering the whole thing before it has had time to fall down. Hot, dry sand preserves things wonderfully well, so many of the buildings in this part of the world are much more complete than those in a damper climate. Sometimes, however, they may have been shaken down by an earthquake or destroyed by an enemy.

Much quicker than this in burying something can be the eruption of a volcano. Pompeii and Herculaneum were two cities near Naples in Italy which were so buried about eighty years after the birth of Christ. They were not deserted cities, either, when the volcano Vesuvius overwhelmed them. Many people died in the disaster so, as the ash and lava has gradually been removed by archaeologists

*The Sphinx, 66ft high, was for many years almost covered in sand*

*Below: a Celtic shield, found in the middle of the Thames near Battersea and probably lost during a river crossing*

*The ruins of Herculaneum, buried in AD 79 under the volcanic ash from Vesuvius. The site has been built over many times. The excavated ruins are in the foreground and the modern city is on the right*

over a number of years, it has been possible to see two Roman towns almost in their original state, even down to food in some of the houses and shops. Volcanic eruptions have covered other towns and villages, too.

Earthquakes, floods and landslides can also destroy and bury towns. Changes of climate, like the coming of an ice age, can cause whole nations to move, leaving the remains of their civilisations, which may be covered over in the course of time by the slow movement of a glacier.

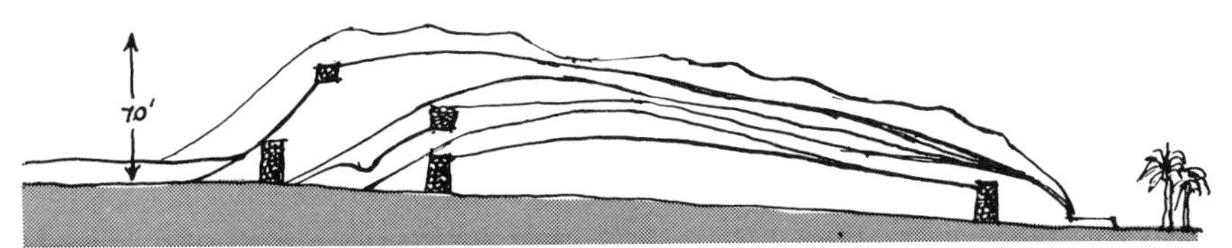


*Diagram of the successive layers of civilisation which built up into the tell of Jericho during the 70,000 years from neolithic to modern times*

History has shown that people over the centuries tend to choose the same sites to build their towns and villages. The spot may be deserted for some years for one reason or another, but after a while someone will build there again, on top of the old and burying it. Gradually a raised area the size or shape of the town or village is formed, which, in the Middle East, is called a tell. A tell can also be formed in a town that is in continuous occupation over a long period. Old buildings are replaced by more modern, which are erected on the old rubble and foundations, so that they are slightly above the level of the previous ones. A tell can indicate the site of an ancient city to an archaeologist.

There are many other ways in which things can vanish. They can be dropped from ships in rivers and seas, or on marshy land, where they sink from sight. And many things have been intentionally buried, like the tombs of the ancient Egyptians, for fear that they would be robbed of their treasures.

*Above: the main trench cut into the tell of Jericho during excavation*

*Below: a model boat buried and preserved in an ancient Egyptian tomb for about 4,000 years*

*Below right: a sacrificial chariot, found dismantled in a bog in Denmark, and reassembled. This dates from about 700 BC*

# How do archaeologists know where to look?

In many cases there may be signs above the ground. These may be part of an old ruin, or perhaps a burial mound. If the ruin is of a large building – a meeting house for instance – the chances are that it was part of a settlement and that there will be the remains of other buildings not far off under the ground. A high, grass-grown mound with a flat top, perhaps many yards across, and with the remains of a defensive ditch all round it and usually situated on high ground, will indicate the presence of a hill fort. Nettles growing in the ditch will make a fort even more likely, as these ditches were also used as rubbish dumps, and nettles like growing in such places.

*Above: the Roman ruins at Leptis Magna in Libya*

*Right: the ramparts of Maiden Castle in Dorset, the most spectacular Iron Age fortress in Britain, destroyed by the Romans*

*Several kinds of electric meter are used in archaeology to discover if anything worth while excavating is buried under the earth. The one shown in the picture is a proton magnetometer. Buried materials have magnetic fields of varying intensity. The magnetometer can distinguish between these and so tell the archaeologist if, for instance, there are iron objects waiting to be discovered some feet below the soil.*

Many old sites are found by chance. Ploughing a field can turn up pieces of bone or pottery, and sometimes more valuable objects. This may mean that the spot was once a village or town. When new roads are built, or land developed for building, mechanical excavators carve huge chunks out of the countryside. In a country as small as England, the building of a motorway can uncover as many as four sites of archaeological interest per mile. Not all of them are of great importance, but teams of amateur archaeologists are being formed to watch what turns up and rescue, or at least photograph and record, what they can.

Earth washed away from the banks of rivers and by floods can reveal things of interest, and sometimes ancient place-names, maps and old legends can give a clue to something that existed in the past. But if nothing is showing above the ground and nothing has been accidentally found, what then?

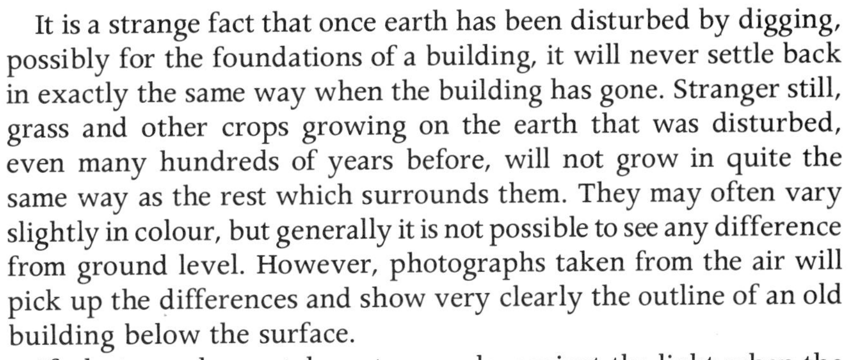

It is a strange fact that once earth has been disturbed by digging, possibly for the foundations of a building, it will never settle back in exactly the same way when the building has gone. Stranger still, grass and other crops growing on the earth that was disturbed, even many hundreds of years before, will not grow in quite the same way as the rest which surrounds them. They may often vary slightly in colour, but generally it is not possible to see any difference from ground level. However, photographs taken from the air will pick up the differences and show very clearly the outline of an old building below the surface.

If photographs are taken at an angle, against the light when the sun is low on the horizon, shadows may show up very slight changes in the level of ground that seems quite flat. If these form a regular pattern, they may also indicate something of archaeological interest. Many important sites have been found by photographing from the air.

*A mass of buried barrow rings revealed from the air by the shadows they cast*

*Above: site of Saxon field system, invisible from the ground, but revealed from the air*

*Right: aerial photography is a quick way of carrying out a first survey, as large areas can be covered in a short time. The survey plane flies on a steady course at a fixed height. At regular intervals a photograph of the ground below is taken, each photograph slightly overlapping the last one. The plane then returns on a parallel course, either to the left or the right, taking more photographs which slightly overlap the sides of the first set, so that the whole area is covered in a series of slightly overlapping squares.*

# Carrying out an excavation

*Below: the plan of a site with a grid marked on it*

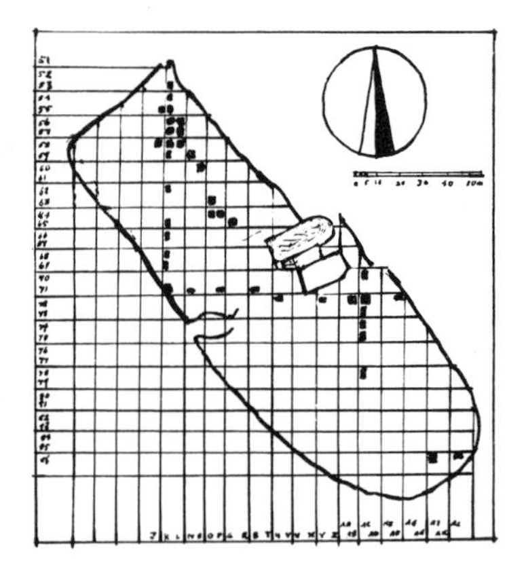

There are so many different kinds of places in which archaeological remains may be found that no one method of excavation will suit them all. Ruins may be in soft earth, in sand, in damp clay or on rocky, boulder-strewn slopes. The buried materials may be fragile, like pottery, or may be walls made of great blocks of stone, or they may be a mixture of the two. In most cases it is not possible to tell exactly what will be found and plans for digging may have to change once the first discovery has been made. As each site presents its own problems, it is not possible to describe them all. One can really only give a general outline of some of the more usual methods.

Once a possible site has been located, perhaps by aerial photography which will outline the main walls, a plan is made of it, which is then marked out on the ground where the digging will take place. It is often also divided up into squares, forming something called a grid, the squares being numbered reference points which help in recording where objects may be found.

*Right: excavation in progress of the Roman Temple of Mithras. The ruins of this temple have been preserved on site, in London*

*Below: using a probe*

Usually trial soundings are made which will help to confirm what is there before digging starts, will show its depth below the surface, and also the kind of ground through which the excavators must dig. These soundings are made with a probe, a long shaft with a screw thread on it and with a hollow end. This is screwed into the ground, the hollow end collecting cores or samples as it pushes into the earth. These can be examined when it is brought up again.

*Left: using a photographic probe to assess whether a tomb is worth excavating*

For exploring a site where it is thought a tomb might be, a special probe is used with a camera and flash-gun built into the end. This is screwed right down until the camera is in the tomb chamber, when a photograph can be taken to discover whether it is worth opening up. But whatever kind of probe is used, soundings must be carried out very carefully to prevent anything important being damaged.

Once the preliminary work has been done and it has been decided to go ahead with the dig, a trial trench with vertical sides is dug at a selected point on the grid. This trench serves two purposes. First it may confirm that there really is something there worth excavating. Secondly, by examining its sides, the archaeologists can see the different soil layers or strata, which will show the sequence of different periods of building or may help to give the date of the site. The layers, some of which may be very thin so that great care is needed in distinguishing one from another, will also show at what level the first building was carried out, as there may well have been several periods in which the same area was used for a town or village. It is important to reach and recognise the very bottom layer if a full history of the place is to be established. Each layer in an excavation is clearly marked by a peg driven into the side of the trench.

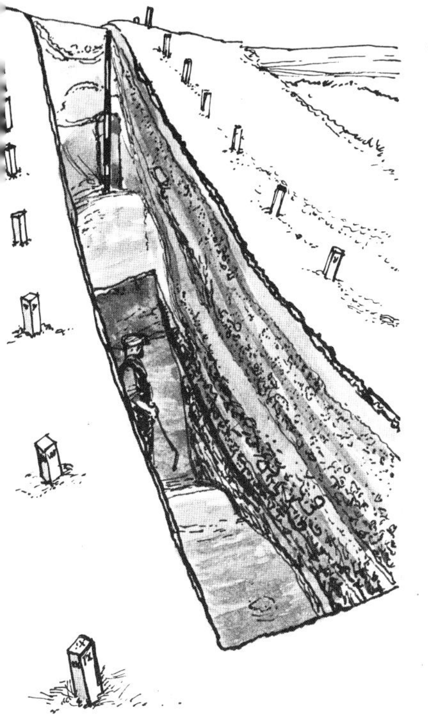

*Left: a trial trench*

The first trench may well have revealed the top of an old wall. Further trial trenches will be dug at other points on the site to confirm what was shown on the photographs and in the soundings. They will confirm, too, the exact position of the building, and they may also show changes in its level, due to the sinking or building up of earth over the years. In other words they are used to continue to build up a picture of what is there and what the work ahead may entail.

*Excavating with trowel and hand shovel*

When the main digging begins, it will probably be done first within one of the squares of the grid, which will in time be worked across systematically. The earth is removed, layer by layer, and taken away to a soil dump well clear of the excavation area. If the trenches have shown that the site is deeply buried, the early digging can be fairly rapid, but greater and greater care is needed as it goes on. For the last part, the work is very slow indeed, and all soil must be sifted to make sure that nothing, however tiny – a bronze pin or a glass bead, perhaps – is missed. Much of the final stage must be carried out with a hand trowel and a small, soft brush, very carefully scraping and brushing the soil away from the old walls and floors, for it is all too easy to destroy very important evidence. A layer of burned earth, only a fraction of an inch thick, may indicate an old hearth or pottery kiln. A pickaxe or spade would wipe it out before anyone knew that it was there.

*Washing potsherds*

*Above: the Wheeler grid system was devised by the British archaeologist Sir Mortimer Wheeler. All digs are marked out and plotted on a grid, but here the lines of the grid are, as it were, left in place as the digging progresses. The grid is first marked on the ground in 5 metre squares and the actual digging is carried out in squares 4 by 4 metres within these, thus leaving a 1 metre wide causeway between each square being excavated. When the whole excavation is complete it is possible, by examining the sides of the undisturbed causeways, to see the changes of level of the earth layers over the whole area. Once this has been recorded the causeways can be removed if it is decided to open up the whole site. In the excavation here illustrated the grid is shown in operation next to an area that has been fully excavated by the same method.*

*Left: surveying a site*

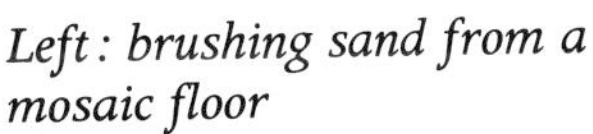

*Left: brushing sand from a mosaic floor*

*Right: measuring the exact position of the find, both horizontally and vertically. The vertical is measured with a plumb line*

Anything of any size that is found, an old pot or a skeleton, for instance, has as much of the surrounding soil as possible removed and is then photographed in the position in which it was discovered. After that it can be moved, but all details about its size and where and how it was found will be very carefully recorded. This recording is done, of course, for all finds of whatever size. Then they are cleaned and stored until they can be given an even more detailed examination.

Samples of soil will be taken where things are found. This is analysed by geologists and chemists to help in the fixing of dates. If there is charcoal present it is particularly useful for this purpose, as it is made up of carbon. Carbon dating is described later on in this book.

Finally, and very important, the archaeologist in charge of the excavation prepares a report, complete with diagrams, drawings and photographs, telling the full story of the work and of what was found on the site. When published, this can be of great help to other archaeologists.

# Chance finds that gave the clue to solving many mysteries

If it is possible to read old writings and inscriptions on things which an archaeologist finds, his task of discovering more about them is much easier. The ancient Egyptians kept written records of many of their activities, first of all on clay tablets and later written on papyrus, a kind of paper made from strips of the stem of the papyrus reed. In painting after painting on the walls of their tombs one can see pictures of scribes at work, taking down details of what was going on.

But how does one read writing in a language thousands of years old and quite forgotten? For a very long time scholars puzzled over the writings of ancient Egypt and got nowhere. Then about two hundred years ago, something happened that gave them the clue.

*Manuscript jar (above) and copper scrolls (below) from Khirbet Qumran*

*Above: near the north-western shore of the Dead Sea, lies Khirbet Qumran. It is a desolate, sun-baked spot and in a deep ravine there, in 1947, in one of the caves that riddle its sides, the first of the Dead Sea Scrolls was found by chance by a young Bedouin shepherd searching for a lost goat. The scrolls were rolls of parchment stored in pottery jars and some contain parts of the Old Testament, probably over 1,000 years older than any known before. Archaeologists were at first unaware of the find and many of the scrolls disappeared. But they were gathered together once more and deciphered. Later excavation produced further scrolls, some of which were on copper.*

*Hieroglyphic*

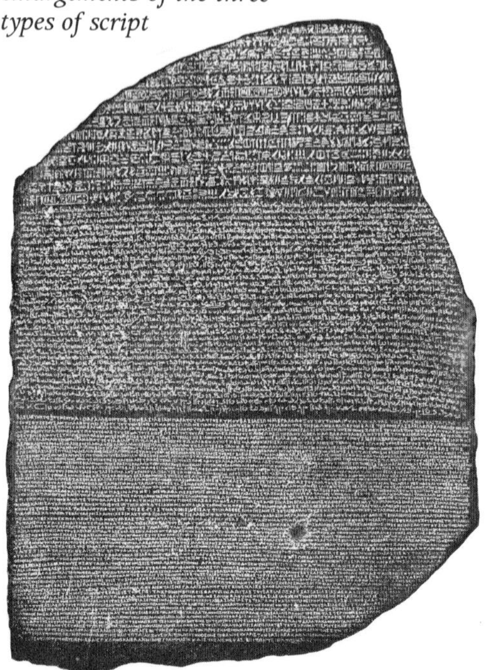

*The Rosetta Stone and enlargements of the three types of script*

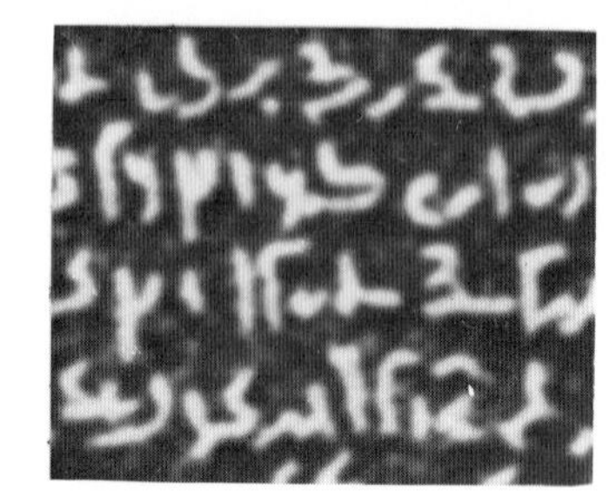

*Demotic*

*Greek*

In 1798 Napoleon invaded Egypt, and the following year some French soldiers were digging fortifications at a place called Rosetta, to the west of the Nile delta. They unearthed a flat slab of stone on which was an inscription in three different kinds of writing. Luckily the officer in charge, Pierre Bouchard, realised that the stone might be important. He guessed that the three inscriptions might, in fact, say the same thing in different languages – and one of them was a known language – Greek.

Copies of the inscriptions were made and studied by scholars all over Europe, but even then it did not turn out to be easy to read the stone. Although it was thought that the general meaning of the texts was the same, they did not correspond word for word. The Egyptians used three forms of writing, hieroglyphics or picture writing, hieratic script which was derived from them, and demotic writing, which was a kind of shorthand. Hieroglyphics and demotic writing appear on the stone, along with the Greek.

The first real break-through was made by a man called Sir Thomas Young, who managed to pick out the name of Ptolemy V, who ruled Egypt in 196 BC. Once Sir Thomas knew how this one word was formed, he began to make some progress, but he did not realise that the ancient Egyptians did not normally use vowels in their writing, and without this knowledge he was once more baffled. Finally it was a young Frenchman, Francois Champollion, who discovered not only this but also realised that many of the Egyptian signs were used to represent *sounds*. The same letter was not always written the same way if the sound of it in speech was different. Once he knew this, he could solve the rest of the puzzle and many of the mysteries about the Egyptian way of life became clear.

The Rosetta Stone is now in the British Museum, London.

*French soldiers find the stone*

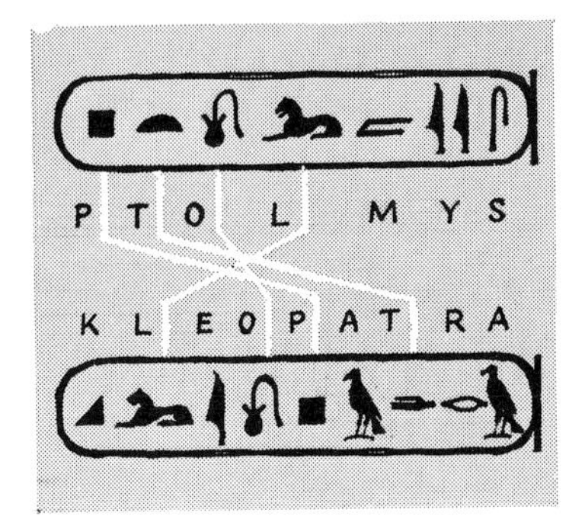


*Above: the key to the hieroglyphic writing on the Stone lies in the names Ptolemy and Cleopatra. Once these few symbols were deciphered, the rest could be worked out*

*Right: paintings on the walls of caves were carried out in prehistoric times. Remarkable cave paintings were discovered by accident at Lascaux in southern France as recently as 1940. The paintings are very skilfully done, and transformed our conceptions of the attitudes and skills of prehistoric man as he lived 15,000 years ago.*

# The rock fortress of Masada

The fortress of Masada stands on the flat top of a great rock, some 1,200 feet high, in the midst of desolate and barren country near the Dead Sea in Palestine. It was the stronghold (30 BC) of Herod the Great, and in it a last dramatic stand was made, 100 years later, against the Roman invaders after the destruction of the Temple of Jerusalem by Titus in AD 70.

To the east there is still a narrow, boulder-strewn path, called the 'snake track', easy to defend because of its narrowness, by which the original inhabitants reached the fort. To the west on the plains below lie the remains of the old Roman siege camps from which, over many months, they tried in vain to breach the walls of the fort. When all else had failed, the Roman commander had an enormous ramp of beaten earth and large stones built, sloping up almost to the level of the outer walls. On top of this he built a wooden siege tower, and against the onslaught of this there was no defence. Rather than be conquered, the remaining heroic defenders killed themselves.

To excavate such a formidable place was an enormous undertaking, but in 1963, backed by the Israeli Government and with help offered by the Israel Defence Forces, and a vast army of volunteers, old and young, from all over the world and from all walks of life, Professor Yigael Yadin set to work. The project required tremendous organisation.

EXCITING FINDS AT MASADA

*The plaited hair of a young woman*

*Leather sandals*

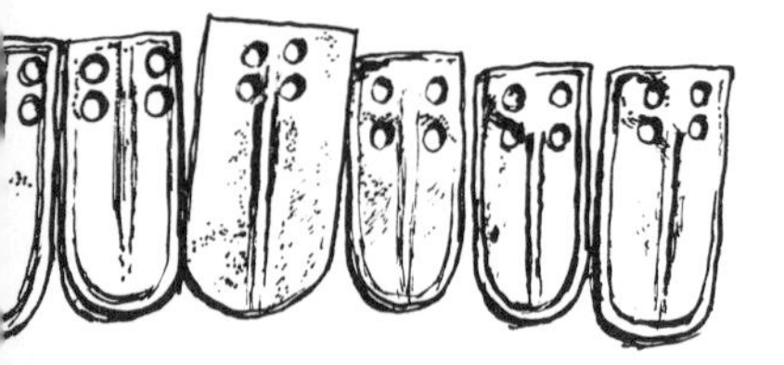

*Silvered armour scales*

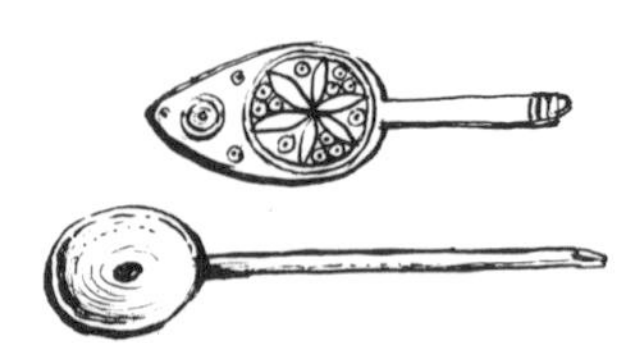

*Ivory egg spoons*

*Front and back of a shekel coin, minted in the year of the Jewish revolt (AD 66)*

*Plaited palm-frond basket*

Above: general view of the rock, showing the Roman camp in the foreground, the ramp behind it and the hanging palace of Herod on the left of the rock

*Close up aerial view (right) and plan (below) of Herod's palace on the edge of the rock*

1 *The Palace Villa*
2 *The large bath-house*
3 *Store rooms*
4 *Gate*

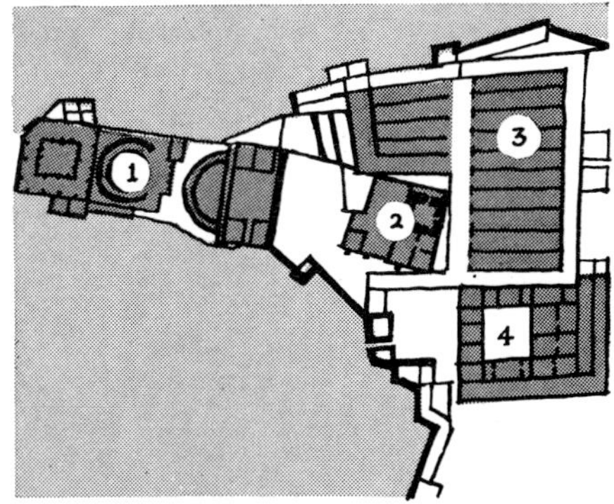

*One of the huge water storage cisterns, carved on the orders of Herod from the solid rock*

A tented camp was set up near the remains of the Roman ramp, and a rough track made up it for the workers to climb each day. Near the top a special wooden stairway had to be built by the army, as the ramp ended below the old walls. Cable-car lines had to be set up to ferry the heavier equipment to the top as no vehicle could make the climb. Special roads were laid for bringing in supplies of food, fuel, tents, tools and so on. Water had to be pumped to the site from quite a distance away and generators for electricity installed. It was almost like the organisation of the Roman siege all over again.

The work went on right into 1965 and many marvellous relics and buildings were discovered, including Herod's own palace, but it must have been one of the most difficult digs ever.

In the midst of that burning desert, the sun in the summer was so hot that the physical work of excavation became impossible. The men and women of the team worked instead on examining and restoring the things they had found. In the winter, icy rain and gales howled around the heights, making work just as much out of the question. Somehow, though, the job was done, a marvellous example of great team-work and a huge amateur volunteer force, which alone made it possible.

# Buried ships

In the long ago past, ships were buried for different reasons. Very often it was believed that their owners could voyage in them to the after life. One of the most famous, the Sutton Hoo Ship, is, however, thought to have been used as a memorial to a seventh century Anglo-Saxon king of East Anglia, for no traces of his actual burial were found in or near it.

*The reconstructed iron helmet from Sutton Hoo*

First signs of the ship were discovered in 1938, when a group of mounds in the county of Suffolk were being examined. Only one man was at work, and he came across some iron bolts. On further investigation, these proved to be from the bow of a huge ship about eighty feet in length.

*One of a pair of hinged gold shoulder-clasps from the Sutton Hoo ship*

*The Sutton Hoo excavation*

A full team of archaeologists began work and they found that, although all the timbers had rotted away, a complete impression of the ship had been left in the soil, clear enough for a plaster cast of it to be made later on. Of the entire structure, only the bolts remained in their original positions, but a most wonderful collection of jewellery, armour – much of it studded with gold – silver bowls and spoons and drinking horns was found.

*Purse lid in gold and enamel from Sutton Hoo, and detail of the enamel design*

Despite the fact that excavation round the Pyramids in Egypt had gone on for many years, it was only in 1954 that a chamber about ninety feet long was discovered under some huge stone blocks, close to the Pyramid of Cheops. This contained all the parts of a one hundred and thirty foot long cedar-wood boat, neatly arranged, ready for assembly. Although they were about 5,000 years old, all the parts, even down to the ropes and sails, were in nearly perfect condition. They had to be especially treated to keep them so, once they were exposed to the air, and the boat is now being assembled and before long will be on view to the public. It is thought that this is the boat in which, after death, the Pharoah would make his journey to eternity.

*Mosaic floor of a Roman villa at Woodchester in Gloucestershire. This was found buried under a churchyard. The holes in the floor were caused by graves being dug right through before it was realised the villa was there. Being in a churchyard, this mosaic is only uncovered once every ten years* (photo: Anthony Kersting)

▲ *The temple at Luxor in Egypt was, like the Sphinx (see page 4), once buried under the sand. The golden mosque in the background was built at what was then thought to be ground level but, when the temple was excavated, it was left high in the air* (photo: Michael Gibson)

▲ *The Temple of Hathor at Denderah, Egypt. On the back wall is the only representation in stone of Cleopatra* (photo: Michael Gibson)

*The Etruscans pre-dated the Romans in Italy. These golden bracelets and diadem date from the 6th and 7th centuries BC and are in the British Museum* ▼ (photo: C. S. Bibbey)

▲ *Cleaning pottery fragments at Guildford Park Manor. A medieval moated manor is being excavated* (photo: Alan Crocker)

▼ *Excavating the moated medieval manor site near Guildford* (photo: Alan Crocker)

▲ *The excavation of the Agora or marketplace at Corinth in progress showing a grid square in the foreground. See the reconstructed Stoa, or covered market, on page 23 for comparison* (photo: Michael Gibson)

*The same grid system in operation at Blackheath, near Guildford, during excavation of a scattering of mesolithic flints.*
▼ *Note the great care used* (photo: Michael Gibson)

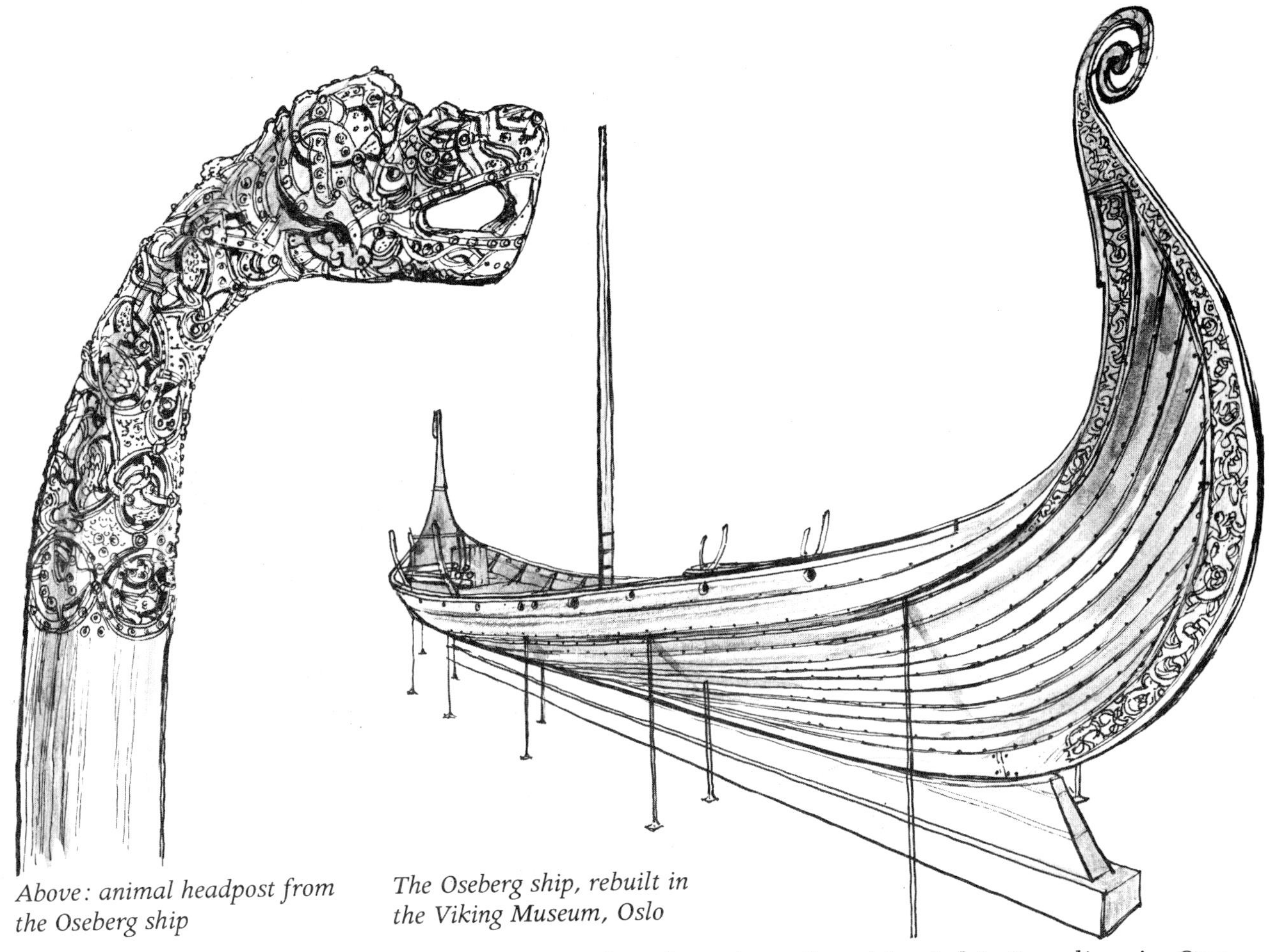

*Above: animal headpost from the Oseberg ship*

*The Oseberg ship, rebuilt in the Viking Museum, Oslo*

A number of ships have been found buried in Scandinavia. One of the best known was found at Oseberg, in Norway. This was a magnificent Viking ship, which it was possible to reconstruct. The Gokstad Ship, found nearby, contained the skeletons of two women.

*Below: the Oseberg ship during excavation*

The blue clay and peat of the area had preserved the timbers of both these boats, but excavating wooden structures from such damp places has special problems. The air begins to dry them out and they will then disintegrate in an incredibly short time, or will be attacked by bacteria. During the unearthing of five Viking ships at the mouth of a fjord on the island of Zealand in Denmark, it was necessary to pump water over them from huge flexible pipes while the work was going on and before they could be properly preserved.

*The golden mask from Mycenae, supposed by Schliemann to be the face of Agamemnon*

# The man who believed the legends

The story of the Trojan wars and the fall of Troy to the ancient Greeks is told in Homer's *Iliad.* Homer was a Greek poet who lived about a thousand years before the birth of Christ, and his wonderful story mixes gods and mortals so that it reads as if it were simply a magnificently told legend.

No one believed that it could be true, or at least based on the truth. No one, that is, until the story was read about one hundred and forty years ago by a schoolboy in Germany called Heinrich Schliemann. He determined that one day he would find the lost city of Troy, but his family was not rich and he was over forty before he had made enough money to carry out his dream. Historians and archaeologists of the time scoffed at his ideas, but nothing would put him off.

His study of the *Iliad* had convinced him that Troy had been situated near the Dardanelles in the north-east corner of Turkey. There was a large tell at a place called Hissarlik that seemed promising and he set to work.

*Right: after his work on the site of Troy, Schliemann, in search of the Tomb of Agamemnon, turned his attention to the ancient citadel of Mycenae in Greece, dating from 1600 to 1200 BC. Here, in 1876, he made one of his most spectacular finds, the shaft graves of a royal cemetery. Inside a circle of stone slabs over eighty feet in diameter he unearthed five tombs containing wonderful treasures, including the golden burial mask which he mistakenly called The Mask of Agamemnon. Later excavations on the site proved him wrong in this, but did little to lessen the magnificence or importance of his discovery. In shaft graves, the dead were buried over the years in layers, one over the top of another, probably with wooden platforms between each burial.*

Heinrich Schliemann

In those days, archaeologists did not have the knowledge and skill that they do now. Their rough methods of digging tended to destroy more than they found, and Schliemann was not even a trained archaeologist. Instead of carefully uncovering the tell, layer by layer, his army of workmen dug with pick and shovel straight into the north-west corner, driving a huge gash into it. Excitement mounted as it was not too long before they found some remains, but they turned out to be Roman of a much later period than the old Grecian Troy. Another cut was begun at the other side of the tell.

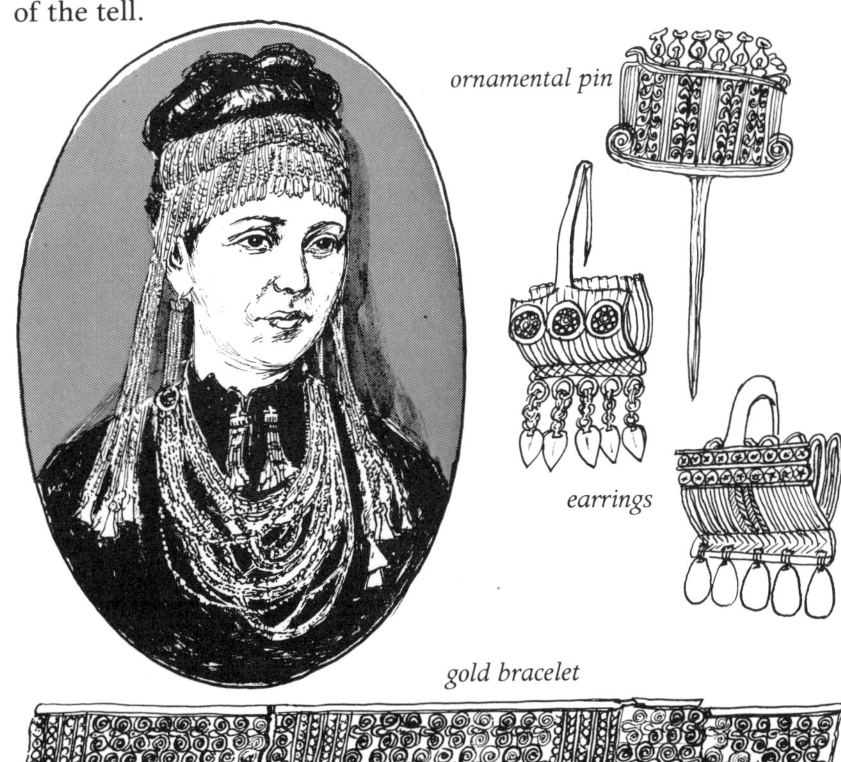


*Right: portrait of Sophia, Schliemann's wife, wearing some of the treasure from Troy, and some of the treasure in detail*

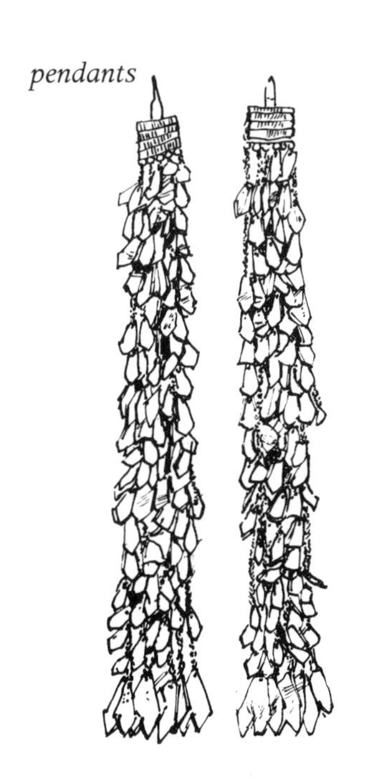


Over many months the digging went on and a number of discoveries showing civilisations of different periods were unearthed, but there was nothing grand enough to convince Schliemann that it could be the remains of Troy. Then at last came triumph – or so Schliemann thought. He found a substantial stone wall, a pair of gates and the ruins of two buildings. Near one of these was a chest which, when opened, revealed more than 8,000 golden objects – beads, necklaces, goblets, bracelets and two diadems. Only Troy, Schliemann was convinced, could have produced such magnificence, and it was indeed a triumph to have found them. It was not until after Schliemann's death that further more scientific excavations showed that, though he had found the site of ancient Troy, he had dug right through it without realising it. The treasure he had found came from an even older civilisation.

# Abu Simbel

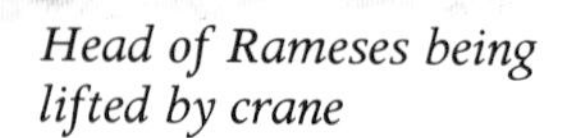
*Head of Rameses being lifted by crane*

*Close-up of small statue of the queen at Ramases' feet*

Sometimes man's progress threatens the destruction of an historical monument of such importance that it cannot be allowed to vanish. Such a thing occurred when the Egyptian government wished to build a gigantic dam, far up the river Nile, at Aswan. The dam would supply desperately needed electrical power, and make possible vast irrigation schemes which would increase the prosperity of the whole country. But if it were built, it would mean flooding a huge tract of the upper Nile valley and submerging for ever some of the most magnificent temples of ancient Egypt. Foremost amongst these was the temple of Rameses II at Abu Simbel.

This temple was a huge structure, carved into the side of a great cliff, the entrance guarded by four enormous seated statues of the pharoah, each one sixty-five feet high. They, too, were carved from the rock face.

Such a treasure from the past simply could not be destroyed, and many schemes were put forward for saving it. Eventually the breathtaking decision was made that the whole temple should be moved to another site, well above the new water level. The Egyptian government alone could not possibly pay for such a huge undertaking, but so concerned were the peoples of the world that many countries banded together and paid money into a fund set up by UNESCO. What had seemed a dream became a possibility.

The task was one requiring the highest degree of engineering skill as well as archaeological knowledge. The most careful and detailed plans were drawn of the whole site and everything on it. A huge concrete frame was built on the top of the cliff, where it had been decided the new home of the temple should be. Then, with infinite patience, the huge stone statues were cut into carefully numbered sections and the reliefs and pillars cut out from the walls with saws. Piece by piece the whole thing was lifted to the cliff top by powerful cranes and fastened to the concrete frame by iron staples. Some time in the distant past the head and upper part of one of the statues had been broken off, and had lain in the sand for as long as anyone could remember. Even this was carefully placed in exactly the same position. Then the concrete frame was filled in to resemble the original cliff.

Many other smaller temples are being saved in the same sort of way. Some, on rather higher ground, may have small dams, known as coffer dams, build round them to hold back the water if it is not going to be too deep. They will be rather like ships in dry-dock.

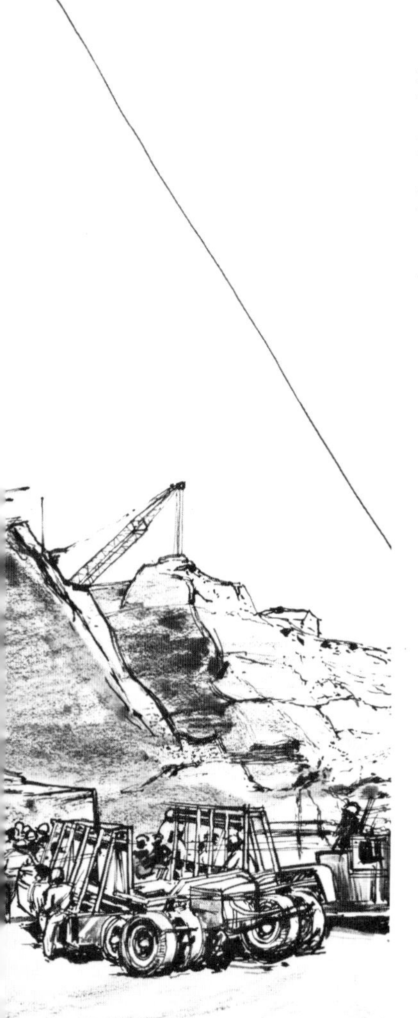

*Above: general view of the site with the work in progress*

*General view of the temple*

*Below: diagram of the coffer dam*

# Rebuilding the past

When several cities have been built, each on the ruins of an earlier one, and archaeologists wish to explore one of the lower ones, they cannot help but destroy something of those on top. Though they may photograph and make written records of what was there, the actual remains are lost for ever.

This is something that cannot be helped, but though archaeologists may, in the course of their work destroy some things, they also sometimes rebuild. When the remains of an old temple or palace are found there may be only a few broken bits of pillar left, or parts of walls no more than a foot or so high. For the archaeologist with his knowledge and experience, this may be enough to tell him just what the building looked like, but to others it may be simply a pile of old stones. So, for the benefit of those who are not experts, a number of buildings are reconstructed.

*Bricks being shaped to replace the originals*

KNOSSOS IN CRETE

*The palace of Knossos dates from the period of the peak of Minoan civilisation in Crete or roughly 1500 years before the birth of Christ. Sir Arthur Evans, who undertook the excavation, carried out extensive restoration to the upper stories of the palace, using concrete in place of rotted timber pillars and broken masonry. The walls of the reception and living rooms had been covered with elaborate frescoes and enough fragments of these remained to enable a number of them to be repainted in something approaching the original style.*

*Above: antechamber to the Royal Apartments in the Palace of Knossos*

*Below: part of a Cretan frieze of athletes with a bull, showing those parts of the plaster which have been filled in during restoration*

*Above: part of the reconstructed staircase in Knossos. The Royal Antechamber, detailed in the adjoining picture, lies behind the 'window' in the top left-hand corner*

*Above: restored triclinium (dining room) at Pompeii*

*Left: reconstruction of the* stoa *of Attalus. A stoa is a covered market, which generally flanks the main market square, or* agora

It is a very slow and painstaking job. First of all, from old writings and drawings, if they exist, and from other buildings from the same period, different parts of which may have survived, information must be assembled to guide the work. If possible, the original materials are used, so that, should there be a jumbled mass of stonework lying about the site – maybe even carved stone ornaments and fragments of wall decoration – all these must be sorted out and pieced together like a jigsaw puzzle. Almost always a lot will be missing, the stone probably taken in the past to make other buildings, and this must be replaced with materials as near to the originals as possible. At the same time, in all archaeological reconstruction, care is taken to mark quite clearly which is new and which is old. People always like to know which is genuine.

*Injecting a glue into plaster to hold it together*

One very famous place where reconstruction has taken place on a large scale is at the Palace of Knossos in Crete, which dates from the very early Greek civilisation there. The work was undertaken by Sir Arthur Evans and, in addition to actual rebuilding, enough fragments of the most wonderful wall paintings were found to enable these to be recreated as well. Today one can really have a very good idea of what the place may have been like in the days of its glory all those years ago.

In Athens, American archaeologists, to make sure that they were using the right material, actually reopened the quarry from which the original marble came, when they were reconstructing the Stoa of Attalus near the Parthenon. A stoa is a covered arcade of shops.

Many of the Greek temples we can see today have been at least partially rebuilt.

*Filling in behind a plaster frieze to anchor it before restoration*

# Exploring under the sea

Men have always sailed the seas, rivers and lakes in their boats and ships. They have carried with them cargoes of things they have made for trade with other countries, or in some cases it might be of rich plunder being brought home from foreign wars.

The ships had living quarters, food, eating and drinking utensils, may have had primitive navigational instruments, and so on – everything needed for a safe voyage, perhaps of many months. They were not, by modern standards, particularly safe vessels. Shipwrecks often occurred, and when one of these boats went to the bottom, it took with it, complete and whole, a small slice of life as it was then lived, and many of its products. Fortunately there was often at least one thing aboard which can nowadays be dated, and the thousands of wrecks under the sea are marvellous hunting grounds for archaeologists.

*Above: raising a statue from the sea-bed*

*This bronze jockey (2nd century BC) was found in the sea off Cape Artemesium near Athens*

*Below: roman amphora being salvaged by a skin diver*

Systematic searching of the sea bottom is, however, a fairly recent branch of archaeology. It is only in the last ten years that breathing, lighting and photographic equipment, and underwater television cameras have been developed that can enable divers to remain and work under water for long periods and at the same time move about reasonably freely.

Many cargoes have been destroyed by the action of salt water or been smashed by storms, and there are worms and shellfish that will burrow into the stone and make their homes in it, gradually destroying it. Metals will corrode, but in many cases the oxides that form on the metals will form a protective coating.

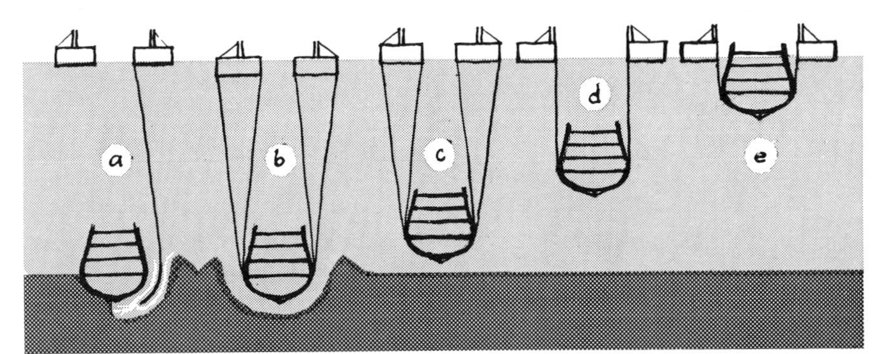


*Right: how the Wasa warship was raised from the sea bed*

*a) Water jets open up six tunnels under the ship to take six double steel cables from the pontoons.*
*b) The pontoons are filled with water and lie almost submerged.*
*c) Water is pumped out of the pontoons, causing them and the Wasa to rise.*
*d) The double six inch cables are replaced by single nine inch cables to reduce pressure on the hull; the hydraulic lifts are transferred to the edge of the pontoons.*
*e) The Wasa breaks surface. Water and mud are pumped out of the hull and she is towed to dry dock for work to continue.*

*Right: lower gun deck of the Wasa*

*Underwater television camera and lighting rig*

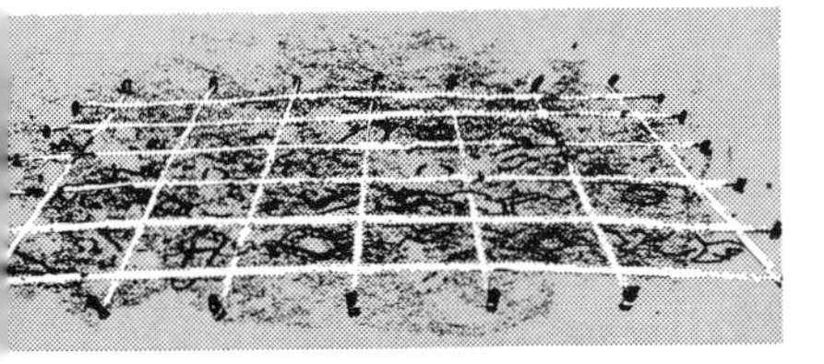

*A grid of plastic tapes on the sea bed, used to mark the position of finds*

The Wasa, a seventeenth century ship, sank in Stockholm harbour in Sweden on her maiden voyage. People tried to raise her cannon almost immediately, but the ship itself stayed in the harbour mud until recently. The hulk, except for the masts, was found to be more or less intact, and was successfully brought up. It contained a lot of interesting belongings of the crew and other equipment, and there was a great deal of carved wood in the structure of the ship itself, which is now being specially treated so that it will be preserved for ever.

There are sunken cities as well as wrecks, which are only now beginning to be explored. Here it is often difficult to tell half-buried, seaweed-encrusted blocks of masonry from natural rocks. Huge compressed-air pumps are needed to clear away the silt.

Some of the most notable finds have been in the Mediterranean Sea. One was the bronze head of Dionysus, Greek ruler of Sicily, found off the coast of Tunisia and now in the Athens Museum, and in 1964 a Celtic ship was discovered off the French coast, laden with weapons and tools.

But perhaps more pottery has been found than anything else. In the Mediterranean, skin-diving holidaymakers can find vases or amphorae (pottery jars for oil, grain and so on) quite easily in certain places, but it is best if they leave them where they are and simply report their finds. Otherwise valuable historical evidence may be destroyed.

# Industrial archaeology

Until comparatively recent times, archaeology was always thought of as dealing only with things that happened many thousands of years ago. Then people began to realise that interesting man-made objects from the last century and even the early part of this one were vanishing as more modern designs took their place. In many cases no record was kept of them, and this was particularly so in the case of early industrial machinery which arrived with the coming of the Industrial Revolution.

Early steam-driven looms and spinning machinery of the cotton mills; primitive beam and pumping engines from the mines; the elaborate hydraulic systems that operated many of the old locks; early railway engines; and farm machines like the first horse-drawn metal ploughs; early radios and navigational aids – all these and many more are of interest to the industrial archaeologist. So too are the quite simple tools that were used in crafts that are dying out. The blacksmith's anvil, the tools of the thatcher, the knife-grinder's treadle wheel are eagerly sought, examined, recorded and, where possible preserved, so that a proper record of man's achievements in these fields is at last being kept. Many of the things go to museums and they can be found almost anywhere a keen searcher can think of – in old barns, on derelict factory sites, abandoned mines, old junk yards. It is a form of archaeology that anyone can join in without any very special training, though it may take some research to find out what some of the things are when you have found them.

*Above: travelling cornmill (19th century) pulled and driven by steam engine*

*Foxton staircase in Leicestershire. This flight of locks has ten chambers which lift boats 75ft*

*In a canal the gates point uphill, against the flow of the water. The water pressure forces the gates together. Water flows into the empty lock when the underground culverts are operated by the ground paddles. The lower gate being closed, the lock fills and when the water pressures are equal on either side, the upper gate can be opened, allowing the boat to enter*

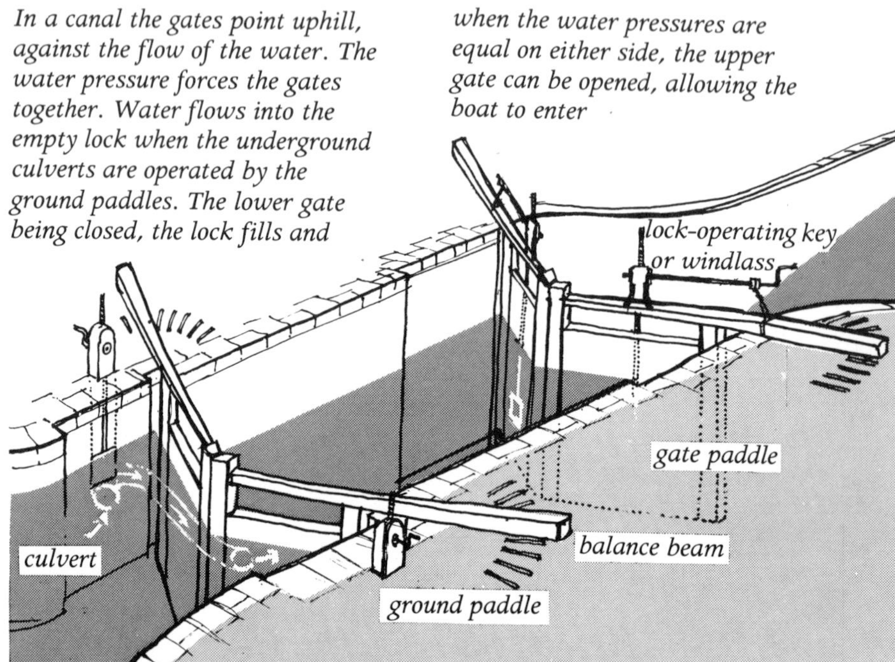

Tower Bridge, built over 78 years ago, is still in perfect working order. Its hydraulic system is powered by two huge steam pumping engines, housed at one end of the bridge

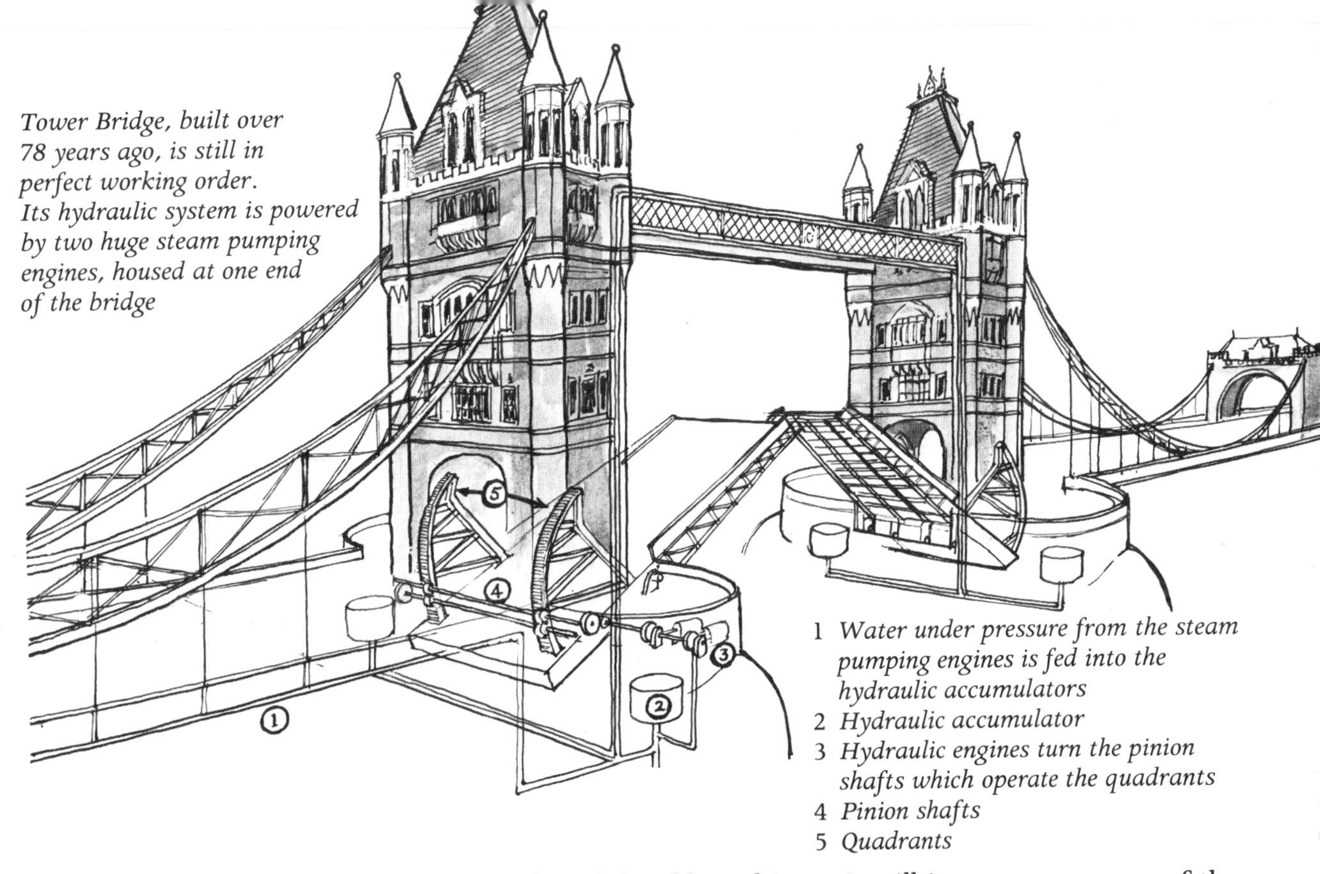


1 Water under pressure from the steam pumping engines is fed into the hydraulic accumulators
2 Hydraulic accumulator
3 Hydraulic engines turn the pinion shafts which operate the quadrants
4 Pinion shafts
5 Quadrants

A tower windmill has a fantail to turn the revolving cap into the wind and a series of gears which transfer the drive down the centre shaft to turn the mill stones

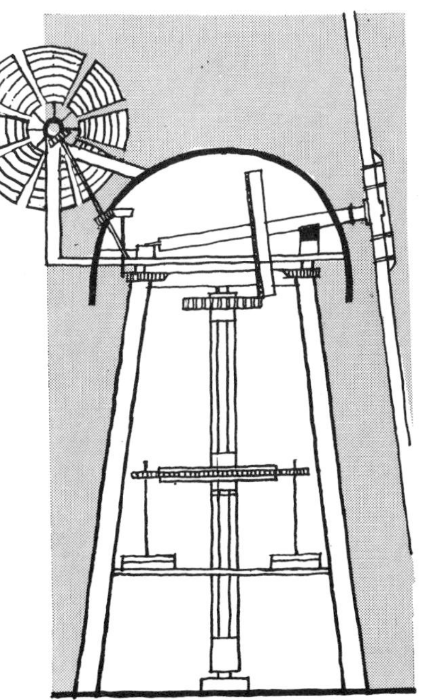

Quite a lot of the old machinery is still in use, as are some of the things it made. The first cast-iron bridge in the world, over the river Severn, the steam-powered Tower Bridge in London, a number of steam locomotives and early cars and bicycles are examples, and the industrial archaeologist will try to make sure that they are never scrapped and are preserved for all time.

It is not, of course, possible to preserve everything, and it is unlikely that even the keenest collector would want to save, for instance, every car that was ever made. The country would be one huge scrap-yard. But carefully chosen samples of the best of each are of value. Preserving them will, in fact, save archaeologists of the distant future a lot of work. We are doing rather what the ancient Egyptians did, though they preserved things, as they thought, for use in after life by people who had died.

WIND AND WATER POWER
*Until the development of steam in the 18th century, man's most powerful machines were driven by harnessing the power of the wind and water*

*Water mill undershot. Water passes through the bottom*

# How do we know how old something is?

*A coin with date or portrait of a known ruler, supplies accurate dating to all nearby finds*

An actual date on a building or on a coin, written records and inscriptions, a particular style of building or architecture, the design of pottery, the technique used to make things and what they have been made of, are all ways of telling how old something is. But most of these depend on comparing them with something else similar, the age of which is already known, perhaps as the result of years of research.

If there is no such clue, science often comes to the rescue. All living material contains a fixed amount of carbon, which is radioactive. It is called Carbon 14, and after death it very slowly disperses by radiation at a uniform rate. If this is measured, it is possible to tell, as far back as 50,000 years ago, when the object containing the carbon died – and hence when it lived. This method of dating is not completely accurate, and can be as much as several hundred years out. For finds which are, say, not more than 1,000 years old, two hundred years can be quite a large error, as one would hope to be able to get within fifty years or even less. However, once one is in the really distant past, 50,000 years ago, before history began, dating cannot expect to be very precise. Two hundred years one way or the other does not matter too much. The error is only one-two-hundred-and-fiftieth of the total years instead of one-fifth.

*Shard (fragment), with name of zealot commander Ben Ya'ir, found at Masada* *(see p. 14)*

*Scarab (brooch made in the form of a beetle) recording the marriage of the Pharaoh Amenophis II to Tiye. The inscription is on the underside*

*Comparing the design on a new found pot with drawings of existing pots*

*Right: varves being formed annually at the bottom of a lake in much the same way as rings grow each year in a tree*

Climate changes, among other things, produce changes in the soil, so that it forms different layers with each change. These were mentioned in the description of carrying out an excavation, and the depth at which something is buried is not as important as identifying the layer in which it was found.

Another way in which differing layers of soil can be formed is by the action of water. The rains of winter and the melting snows from the mountains and high land in spring wash down silt into the rivers and lakes. Each year a layer of this silt, called a varve, is deposited on the bottom of the lakes. The layers do not merge completely into one, and if an object is found buried in a dried-out lake bed, it is possible to tell how old it is by counting the varves above it. They form much in the same way the rings form in the trunk of a tree, one each year, and the tree rings can also be useful in establishing the age of timber.

*Above: grains of plant pollen can survive amazingly well. A particular pollen indicates the plant growing at the time, which in turn indicates the climate, which indicates the period of pre-history*

*Right: a radio-carbon dating laboratory. New scientific techniques used to find out about the past*

# What you, yourself, can do

*Field walking and things you may find. Get permission from the owner of the land first*

Most of the activities described in this book so far are ones carried out by skilled archaeologists. Some can be done, and are done, by amateurs with a fair archaeological knowledge and enough spare time to travel, and money to buy the necessary equipment. But what of someone who wants to learn about archaeology, lives at home and has little money to spare, someone who is, perhaps, still at school? Is there anything that he or she can do? There is; a great deal.

A start has been made by reading this book, and there are many others which can be bought, or borrowed from libraries. Some treat the subject in a very simple way, and you can progress to the more difficult in time. National and local museums contain wonderful collections of archaeological finds and often have permanent demonstrations set up, showing how archaeologists go about their work. Museum curators and their assistants will always be glad to help and advise anyone who is really keen. Should you find something that you think may be of historical interest – a fossil, old coin or a piece of pottery, for instance, your local museum is the place to take it to find out about it.

Look for such things in the beds or in the banks of streams, or in fields which have been recently ploughed (asking the owner for permission first). Ploughing often turns up something, but it is best to look after rain, which will have helped to wash away mud which would be likely to obscure something as small as a coin.

Such finds will be made more or less by chance, and even if you make careful notes of where you found something lying, an expert will still have difficulty in telling you how old it is. So much depends on where it was originally buried and the layer in which it lay. To find really worthwhile things, it is best by far to form an archaeological club in your school or with friends, and enlist help from your museum. They may have old maps which can be studied and which can give a guide to the most likely places to start looking, and so save a great deal of time. And equally important, if you do discover something worthwhile, they will show you how to excavate it in the proper way so that nothing is destroyed.

Join your county or town archaeological society. Through them you can learn what excavations are going on in your own area and in other parts of the country, where volunteer helpers are often needed. On many sites, anyone who is keen is welcome. Whole parties of schoolchildren help every year on many important digs during their holidays, living in tents on the site itself. This can be the best way of all to learn what it is all about, but the visits must be properly planned and agreed with the site director first. Do not just turn up.

*Searching the river bank is a likely way to start*

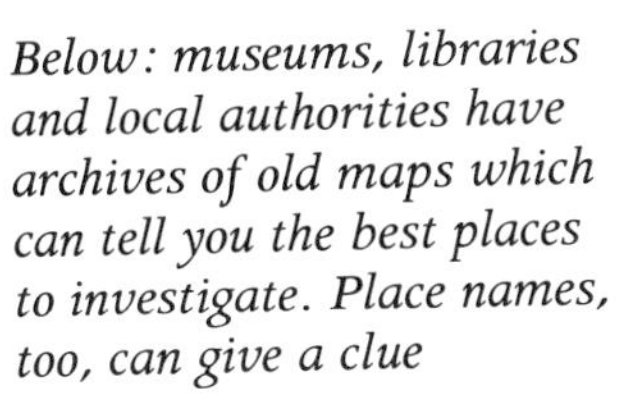

*Below: museums, libraries and local authorities have archives of old maps which can tell you the best places to investigate. Place names, too, can give a clue*

FLINT MINING

*Flints occur naturally in areas of chalk downland. Sometimes there were seams of flint nodules buried in the chalk. Neolithic man sank a shaft until the flint was reached, and then worked outwards into the seam. The shafts were about 15 feet across by 20 feet deep. But even so the underground tunnels and galleries were extensive enough to need oil lamps so that the workers could see.*

*The picture on the right shows the gallery openings at the bottom of an excavated mine at Grimes Graves, the most famous mines in England, on the Suffolk/Norfolk border.*

One of the most common things that can be found, especially on chalk downs, are flints. They can, like coins and pieces of pottery, be turned up by ploughing, and another good place to look for them is in the scrapings of rabbit burrows. But it is not always very easy to tell whether they are ones that have been 'worked' by early man. If they are in the definite shape of something such as an arrow-head or hand-axe, there is no great problem, but scrapers and knives are much less easy to distinguish.

Early flints were worked by striking them with a stone hammer so that flakes flew off, leaving a sharp cutting edge. The flakes themselves would in turn be shaped for smaller tools. But frost can crack a flint, leaving sharp-edged pieces, so one has to know just what to look for. If a flint has a fairly regular pattern of flaking round its edge, it is likely to have been worked, and some of the other indications are shown and described in the pictures and captions.

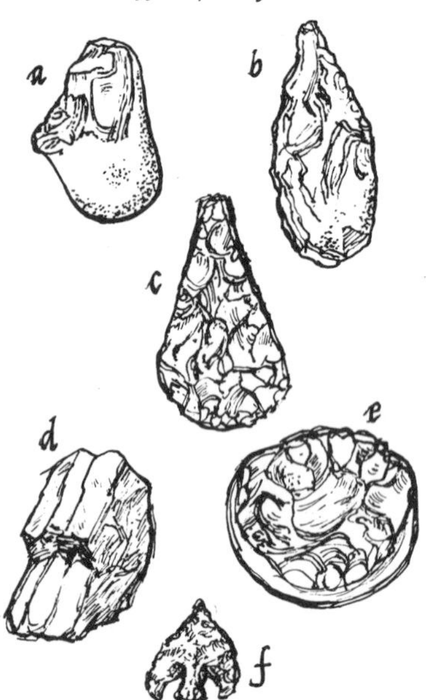


A SELECTION OF THE FLINTS YOU MIGHT FIND

*a) early paleolithic pebble tool*
*b) Abbevillian axe*
*c) middle Archeulian axe*
*d) paleolithic/mesolithic core-tool (a sort of plane)*
*e) Beaker culture disc knife, with polished edge*
*f) tanged and barbed arrowhead*

OTHER BOOKS YOU MIGHT LIKE TO READ

Bray, Warwick and Trump, David. A DICTIONARY OF ARCHAEOLOGY, *Penguin Books.*
Ceram, C. W. GODS, GRAVES AND SCHOLARS, *Gollancz.*
Coles, John. FIELD ARCHAEOLOGY IN BRITAIN, *Methuen.*
Eydoux, Henri-Paul. IN SEARCH OF LOST WORLDS, *Hamlyn.*
James, T. G. H. THE ARCHAEOLOGY OF ANCIENT EGYPT, *Bodley Head.*
Magnusson, Magnus. INTRODUCING ARCHAEOLOGY, *Bodley Head.*
Magnusson, Magnus. THE VIKING EXPANSION WESTWARDS, *Bodley Head.*
McEvedy, Colin. THE PENGUIN ATLAS OF ANCIENT HISTORY, *Penguin Books.*
Osborn, Jane. STONE AGE TO IRON AGE, *Longman.*
Place, Robin. PREHISTORIC BRITAIN, *Longman.*
Woods, Eric S. COLLINS FIELD GUIDE TO ARCHAEOLOGY IN BRITAIN, *Collins.*